AI Transformation, Ensuring Human Priorities in the Age of Automation

The Scandinavian Way

By Martin Meller

In a world where AI often knows more about us than we do, let's hope it has the decency to at least pretend it's surprised by our choices.

Imprint: Independently published

For more information about "AI Transformation, Ensuring Human Priorities in the Age of Automation", you may contact Meller Consult ApS.

Email: info@meller-consult.com
Homepage: www.meller-consult.com

AI Transformation, Ensuring Human Priorities in the Age of Automation

The Scandinavian Way

Introduction to AI transformation

In the labyrinth of today's business world, Artificial Intelligence (AI) emerges not just as a tool, but as a pivotal architect reshaping landscapes. Its influence spans across sectors, from automating mundane tasks to pioneering innovations. Yet, amidst this technological crescendo, a question lingers – how do we ensure that this digital symphony resonates with human priorities?

AI, in its essence, is a mirror reflecting our ingenuity, a tool that, when wielded with foresight, can amplify human potential. Its impact is profound and multifaceted. In the realm of customer experience, AI has redefined personalization, enabling businesses to tailor services with precision that was once the stuff of science fiction. In operations, predictive analytics and automation have streamlined processes, carving out spaces for creativity and strategic thinking.

However, this digital dawn is not without its shadows. The rapid integration of AI has sparked concerns – from ethical dilemmas to the fear of job displacement. It's a tightrope walk between embracing efficiency and nurturing the human core of businesses.

This book, at its heart, is a compass guiding leaders through the AI landscape, ensuring that human values are not lost in the digital abyss. It aims to demystify AI, presenting it not as an adversary, but as an ally in building a future where technology and humanity enhance each other.

The objectives are clear:

1. **Illuminate the path**: Provide a clear understanding of AI's role in business, cutting through the fog of jargon to reveal its true potential and limitations.

2. **Human-centric approach**: Champion a Scandinavian-inspired leadership model that places employee well-being and ethical considerations at the forefront of AI adoption.

3. **Practical wisdom**: Offer actionable strategies and real-world case studies, illustrating how businesses can harness AI while staying true to human-centric values.

4. **Future-Proofing**: Equip leaders with the foresight to navigate the evolving AI landscape, preparing them for emerging trends and challenges.

In essence, this book is a dialogue between technology and humanity, a narrative that champions balance, where AI is a tool for empowerment, not replacement. It's about writing a future where machines augment human potential, and businesses thrive on the bedrock of ethical, people-focused values.

Embracing AI in business: because who doesn't want a digital overlord that's better at your job than you are?

Developing an AI strategy and principles

A robust AI strategy and its guiding principles stands as a cornerstone for a successful AI transition. This chapter delves into the intricate process of crafting an AI vision and mission that resonates with the company's core ethos, outlining guiding principles that navigate the ethical and practical aspects of AI implementation, and intricately linking this strategy to the overarching business objectives.

The landscape of AI in business is not just a tale of technological triumph but a narrative interwoven with ethical considerations, strategic foresight, and human-centric approaches. As we embark on this exploration, we will uncover how a well-articulated AI vision and mission can serve as a beacon, guiding companies through the complex maze of AI integration. We will delve into the art of developing guiding principles that ensure AI initiatives are not only technologically advanced but also ethically sound and socially responsible.

Moreover, the chapter will emphasize the criticality of aligning AI strategies with business strategies, ensuring that AI is not an isolated venture but a harmonious extension of the business's core objectives and values. This alignment is pivotal in realizing the full potential of AI, transforming it from a mere tool into a strategic ally that propels businesses towards innovation, efficiency, and sustainable growth.

Through real-world examples, practical insights, and a focus on Scandinavian leadership styles, this chapter aims to equip business leaders, those in Denmark, the EU, and beyond, with the knowledge and tools to navigate the AI landscape effectively. It will provide a comprehensive understanding of how to create AI strategies that are not only technically proficient but also ethically grounded and strategically aligned with long-term business goals.

As we journey through this chapter, we will explore how AI, when strategically harnessed and guided by strong principles, can be a transformative force, reshaping businesses, and industries in profound ways. Let's embark on this journey to understand how to develop AI strategies and principles that are not just about embracing new technologies but about fostering a future where technology and humanity converge for the greater good.

Crafting the AI vision

The AI vision of a company is more than a statement; it's a narrative that encapsulates the future aspirations and the role AI plays in achieving them. It's about envisioning a future where AI acts as a catalyst for growth, innovation, and positive change.

Vision as inspiration and direction: The vision should inspire not just the leadership but every stakeholder in the company. For example, a tech firm aspiring to be a leader in ethical AI solutions is not just setting a goal but is also defining the path it intends to tread. This vision should be communicated in a way that every employee, from developers to salespersons, understands their role in achieving it.

Realistic and forward-looking: While being ambitious, the vision must also be rooted in the realm of possibility. It should account for the current state of AI technology and its potential evolution. For instance, envisioning AI applications that respect user privacy and data security in a tech firm aligns with both ethical standards and technological trends.

Make it tangible: Each employee need to envision themselves into the vision to ensure a buy-in by all groups. This should be done by creating a narrative with real use cases explaining how their world, their business, and their task would be in e.g. 3 years when an AI transformation is fully implemented making it real for the employee groups explaining the advances and benefits which will come true in the future.

Formulating the AI mission

The AI mission is where the vision gets translated into a tangible set of objectives. It's a commitment to leveraging AI in ways that align with the company's broader goals and values.

Defining the 'Why' and 'How': The mission should clearly articulate why AI is important for the organization and how it will be used to achieve specific goals. For a healthcare provider, this could mean integrating AI to personalize patient care, thus directly linking AI use to improved patient outcomes and satisfaction.

Actionable and measurable: The mission should lead to actionable strategies. It's not just about lofty ideals but about practical steps that can be taken. For example, the mission might involve investing in AI research and development, partnering with AI ethics boards, or training staff in AI technologies.

Aligning with core values: The mission should reflect the company's core values. If a company values innovation, its AI mission might focus on using AI to drive new product developments. If it values customer satisfaction, the AI mission might center around enhancing customer service through AI-driven insights.

Creating an AI vision and mission is a critical and initial step in AI transformation. It requires a deep understanding of the company's aspirations, capabilities, and values. By crafting a vision that is both inspiring and realistic, and a mission that is actionable and aligned with core values, companies can set a solid foundation for their AI journey. This foundation not only guides the company's AI initiatives but also ensures that these initiatives contribute meaningfully to the company's overall success and ethos.

Ethical AI principles

Developing ethical AI principles is important in ensuring that AI technologies are used responsibly and all employees have a beacon that can guide them in autonomously utilize AI's for individual purposes without each time getting IT/Legal/upper managements approval. These principles serve as a moral framework guiding every aspect of AI development and deployment.

Fairness and non-discrimination: AI systems should be designed to be fair and not discriminate against any group or individual. For example, an automotive manufacturer implementing AI in autonomous vehicles must ensure that the AI's decision-making process is free from biases that could lead to discriminatory outcomes. This involves rigorous testing and validation of AI algorithms to ensure they treat all users equitably.

Accountability and responsibility: There should be clear accountability for AI decisions. This means if an AI system makes a decision that negatively impacts users, there should be a transparent process to determine why it happened and who is responsible. For instance, in healthcare AI applications, there must be clarity on how decisions were reached and who is accountable for those decisions – the AI developers, the healthcare providers, or both.

Transparency and explainability: AI systems should be transparent and their decisions explainable. Users should be able to understand how and why a particular AI decision was made. For a financial services company using AI for credit scoring, this means being able to explain to customers how the AI model assesses their creditworthiness.

Sustainability and inclusivity

Incorporating sustainability and inclusivity into AI principles ensures that AI solutions are developed with a long-term perspective, considering their impact on the environment and society.

Environmental sustainability: AI solutions should be designed with environmental sustainability in mind. For a renewable energy company, this could mean using AI to optimize energy distribution in a way that maximizes renewable energy use and minimizes carbon footprint. It involves developing AI models that are not only energy-efficient in their operation but also contribute to broader environmental goals.

Inclusivity and accessibility: AI should be accessible to and inclusive of diverse user groups. This involves designing AI systems that are user-friendly for people with different abilities and backgrounds. For instance, an AI-powered educational platform should be accessible to users with disabilities, offering features like voice commands, screen readers, and other assistive technologies.

Cultural sensitivity: AI systems should be culturally sensitive and respect the diversity of users. This means considering different cultural contexts in AI design and ensuring that AI applications do not perpetuate cultural stereotypes or biases.

Developing guiding principles for AI implementation is about ensuring that AI technologies are used in a way that is ethical, sustainable, and inclusive. These principles should be deeply ingrained in the company's AI strategy, reflecting its commitment to using AI as a force for good – enhancing safety, fairness, and efficiency while respecting ethical boundaries and societal values. By adhering to these principles, companies can not only avoid the pitfalls of unethical AI use but also build trust with their stakeholders and contribute positively to society.

Linking AI strategy to business strategy

Strategic alignment. Integrating AI strategy with business strategy is not just about adopting new technologies; it's about aligning these technologies with the core objectives and values of the business.

Supporting key business objectives: AI initiatives should directly contribute to the primary goals of the business. For example, if a retail chain aims to enhance customer satisfaction, its AI strategy could focus on personalization algorithms that recommend products based on individual customer preferences and purchase history. This alignment ensures that AI is not just a technological showpiece but a tool that drives tangible business outcomes.

Customized AI solutions: The AI strategy should be tailored to the specific needs and challenges of the business. In a logistics company, for instance, AI could be used to optimize supply chain management, reducing costs and improving delivery times. This customization ensures that AI solutions are relevant and effective in addressing the unique challenges of the business.

Long-term perspective. A forward-looking AI strategy is essential for sustainable growth and adaptability in a rapidly evolving technological landscape. It is not about "betting" on *one* technology like ChatGPT as you do not know what will be launched tomorrow, make the strategy and definition focused on principles and directions.

Investing in future-ready AI: Businesses should invest in AI technologies that are scalable and adaptable to future needs. For a financial institution, this might mean deploying AI systems for predictive analytics that can evolve with changing market conditions and regulatory environments.

Continuous learning and adaptation: The AI strategy should include provisions for ongoing learning and adaptation. This involves regularly updating AI models, incorporating new data, and staying abreast of advancements in AI technology. For a pharmaceutical company, this could mean continuously improving AI-driven drug discovery processes to keep pace with scientific advancements.

Employee involvement and leadership commitment

The success of an AI strategy is heavily dependent on the people behind it – from the leadership driving the vision, to the middle managers who sets the prioritization in the operational units, to the employees implementing and interacting with AI systems.

Encouraging employee participation: Employees should be encouraged to contribute ideas and feedback on AI initiatives. This could involve setting up innovation labs or suggestion schemes where employees can propose AI solutions for various business challenges. For instance, in an energy company, employees could suggest AI applications for optimizing renewable energy production, or employees suggesting an automated meeting transcript bot to ensure meeting minutes and actions points with deadlines are done automatically.

Leadership driving AI culture: Leadership commitment is crucial in fostering a culture that embraces AI. This means leaders should not only endorse AI initiatives but also actively participate in them. For example, the CEO might personally involve in AI projects, demonstrating a commitment to innovation and leading by example.

Training and development: Investing in employee training and development is key to ensuring that the workforce is equipped to work alongside AI. This could include AI literacy programs, workshops on ethical AI use, and opportunities for hands-on experience with AI tools.

Linking AI strategy to business strategy is a multifaceted process that requires strategic alignment, a long-term perspective, and active involvement from both leadership and employees. By ensuring that AI initiatives are in harmony with the overall business goals and values, companies can leverage AI as a powerful tool for growth, innovation, and competitive advantage.

Developing an AI strategy and principles is a multifaceted process that requires a clear vision, strong ethical foundations, and strategic alignment with business goals. By adhering to these guidelines, companies can ensure that their journey in AI transformation is not only technologically advanced but also ethically sound and strategically effective.

Mental blocks in AI transformation

In the transformative journey towards integrating Artificial Intelligence (AI) in business, a significant hurdle often lies not in the technology itself, but in the mindset of those who lead and operate within these organizations. Leaders and employees face a myriad of mental barriers that can impede the adoption and effective utilization of AI technologies. These barriers, deeply rooted in human nature and organizational culture, often manifest as:

Fear of the unknown: AI, a complex and evolving field, can intimidate those unfamiliar with its mechanisms. This fear is often compounded by concerns over job security and the perceived threat of AI to traditional roles.

Resistance to change: Humans are creatures of habit, and introducing AI disrupts established routines and processes, leading to resistance. This resistance is not just a reluctance to adopt new technology but also a defense of familiar, comfortable practices.

Overwhelm by complexity: The intricacies of AI can be overwhelming, especially for those without a technical background. This complexity can lead to a sense of helplessness or defeatism, hindering engagement with AI initiatives.

Ethical and privacy concerns: With AI's ability to process and analyze vast amounts of data, concerns about ethical implications and privacy breaches naturally arise. These concerns can lead to scepticism and apprehension towards AI adoption.

Strategies to overcome these blocks

Addressing these mental barriers requires a multifaceted approach, combining education, inclusive change management, appreciations of failures, play, ethical transparency, and a focus on human-AI collaboration:

Demystifying AI: Simplifying AI concepts and demonstrating its practical applications can alleviate fears and misconceptions. Educational initiatives should be tailored to different levels of understanding, making AI accessible to all.

Inclusive change management: Involving employees in the AI transformation process fosters a sense of ownership and control. This approach aligns with Scandinavian leadership values of egalitarianism and collaboration, easing the transition to new technologies.

Addressing ethical concerns: Establishing clear ethical guidelines and transparent data practices reassures employees and builds trust. This approach is in line with the Scandinavian emphasis on integrity and ethical responsibility.

Celebrating Human-AI collaboration: Highlighting examples where AI enhances human capabilities can shift the perception of AI from a threat to an ally. Showcasing success stories where AI has augmented human work can inspire and motivate employees.

Embracing failures and play: No one knows where the AI journey will end, and as a company it is important to foster an atmosphere of openness to explore the new technologies possibilities and getting the employees to play around with the technology. Explore and innovate thereby finding new and game changing ways to develop the business. But, it is also important to remember that not everything will be successful, so embrace the failures and errors which will happen and take them as learning steps towards a future breakthrough.

Understanding and addressing these mental barriers is crucial for successful AI integration in businesses. It ensures that AI transformation is not just a technological shift but also a cultural and mindset change, aligning with the core values of Scandinavian leadership. By overcoming these barriers, organizations can harness the full potential of AI, fostering innovation, efficiency, and a more engaged workforce.

Case Studies and Examples

Danske Bank, Denmark: Danske Bank's AI-driven fraud detection system involved employees in its development and implementation. This inclusive approach not only improved the system's effectiveness but also fostered a culture of trust and collaboration around AI.

IKEA, Sweden: IKEA's use of AI in inventory management and customer service demonstrates AI augmenting human work. Employee training in AI systems led to improved efficiency and job satisfaction.

KONE, Finland: KONE's AI implementation for predictive maintenance in elevators and escalators involved technicians in the integration process. This approach enhanced service efficiency and employee engagement, showcasing the benefits of human-AI collaboration.

Identifying AI projects

In the transformative landscape of AI integration in businesses, the identification of the right problems to solve is crucial. This chapter unfolds the intricate process of discerning which AI projects to undertake, a phase vital for leveraging AI's power in augmenting efficiency, decision-making, and customer fulfillment. Our approach, inspired by Scandinavian leadership, emphasizes egalitarianism and employee well-being, ensuring that AI serves a purpose beyond mere technological advancement.

Why is it critical to identify the right AI projects

The significance of identifying apt AI projects lies in aligning technology with strategic business goals. The challenge for businesses is navigating the plethora of potential AI applications and selecting those that yield the most significant benefits. Overcoming this challenge involves a methodical approach, combining data analysis with a deep understanding of business processes and stakeholder needs.

AI project identification in practice

In-Depth business process analysis

Many businesses grapple with identifying the specific areas where AI can deliver transformative impacts. This challenge stems from the difficulty in recognizing processes within their operations that are ripe for AI enhancement.

A compelling approach is exemplified by a manufacturing company that revolutionized its supply chain through AI. By employing meticulous process mapping and bottleneck identification, the company can highlight specific areas for AI intervention, thereby enhancing their operational workflow.

The key lies in developing comprehensive process maps that detail every step of a business operation. AI is then utilized to sift through these maps, analyzing data meticulously to unearth inefficiencies and areas ripe for improvement. This process of detailed analysis allows for the targeted application of AI solutions where they are most needed.

The result is a substantial enhancement in operational efficiency and a streamlined process flow. This approach ensures that AI is applied in a manner that directly contributes to the business's core operational goals.

The essence of successful AI implementation lies in a thorough and detailed analysis of business processes. Understanding the intricacies of these processes is fundamental to identifying the most impactful areas for AI application.

The employee perspective in AI integration

A primary concern in AI integration is to ensure it complements rather than disrupts existing employee roles and operations. The challenge is to integrate AI in a way that aligns with and supports the workforce.

A solution that has proven effective, particularly in retail environments, is the active engagement of employees through structured discussions. This method allows employees to contribute their insights and ideas on how AI can enhance inventory management systems.

The process involves the implementation of digital tools designed for continuous employee feedback and direct observation. These tools allow for the collection of real-time data from employees, offering a clearer picture of how AI can be integrated seamlessly into their daily workflows.

By adopting this approach, AI solutions developed are more in tune with the practical realities of on-ground operations. It ensures that AI integration is both practical and beneficial from an employee's perspective.

Employee involvement is not just beneficial but essential for the practical and effective integration of AI in business processes. Their insights provide valuable guidance on how AI can be utilized to enhance, rather than disrupt, existing operations.

Understanding the customer perspective

Aligning AI initiatives with customer expectations is a significant challenge. Businesses must ensure that their AI strategies resonate with and fulfill customer needs.

An effective approach is the systematic collection and analysis of customer feedback, as seen in the banking sector. Here, AI has been employed to refine customer service, tailoring it to meet and exceed customer expectations.

This involves the development of comprehensive mechanisms for feedback collection, followed by the integration of these customer insights into AI development. The aim is to ensure that AI solutions are shaped by a deep understanding of customer needs and preferences.

AI solutions developed through this approach lead to a marked enhancement in customer satisfaction and loyalty. They are tailored to meet the specific needs and expectations of customers, thereby fostering a more engaging and satisfying customer experience.

Customer feedback is an invaluable asset in the development of customer-centric AI solutions. It is the cornerstone of AI strategies that are truly aligned with customer needs and preferences.

Technical complexity and feasibility assessment

Ensuring the technical viability and feasibility of AI solutions is a multifaceted challenge. It requires a comprehensive understanding of both the technological capabilities and the practical aspects of implementation.

A collaborative approach, akin to what is observed in healthcare AI applications, involves the joint efforts of IT specialists, data scientists, and key business stakeholders. Together, they assess the technical requirements, data availability, and practical potential of AI solutions.

This collaboration extends to conducting in-depth data quality assessments and pilot studies for testing concepts. These steps are crucial in determining the technical feasibility and potential impact of AI applications.

The outcome of this rigorous process is the development of AI solutions that are not only technically sound but also ethically compliant and practically viable.

Comprehensive feasibility studies are the bedrock of successful AI projects. They ensure that AI solutions are developed with a clear understanding of their technical capabilities and practical implications.

Making the business case for AI

Articulating and demonstrating the return on investment (ROI) of AI initiatives is a critical challenge for businesses. It involves not only showcasing the financial benefits but also the broader impacts on operations and brand value.

The solution lies in ROI-focused prioritization and in-depth cost-benefit analysis. This approach is exemplified in the logistics industry, where AI-driven route optimization has been shown to yield significant financial and operational benefits.

The process involves the development of a prioritization matrix, coupled with comprehensive risk assessments. This matrix helps in evaluating and ranking AI initiatives based on their potential ROI, while risk assessments ensure that potential challenges and obstacles are identified and mitigated.

The result is the strategic and profitable investment in AI, where initiatives are chosen not just for their technological prowess but for their tangible contributions to business growth and efficiency.

Developing a well-structured business case for AI is imperative. It is the foundation for justifying AI investments and ensuring that they align with and contribute to the overarching business objectives.

Tools and techniques for problem identification

Selecting the appropriate tools for identifying AI opportunities within a business can be daunting. The challenge is to choose tools that effectively uncover areas where AI can be most beneficial.

The solution involves the utilization of advanced data analytics, AI readiness assessment tools, and interactive workshops for ideation. This combination of analytical and collaborative methods ensures a comprehensive approach to problem identification.

Implementing a blend of these tools and techniques allows for a more nuanced and thorough exploration of potential AI applications. It enables businesses to identify opportunities that align with their specific objectives and market demands.

The outcome of this multifaceted approach is the identification of AI opportunities that are strategically aligned with business goals and market needs.

A comprehensive approach, combining both analytical and collaborative methods, is essential for effective problem identification in AI. It ensures that AI opportunities are identified in a manner that aligns with the strategic objectives and practical realities of the business.

Case study: Amazon

In our exploration of AI transformation, Amazon stands as a quintessential example, a testament to the transformative power of AI in business. Why Amazon? Simply because it epitomizes how a company, originally a book-selling platform, morphed into a global AI-driven powerhouse. This case study is a beacon for any business venturing into AI, showcasing not just the successes but also the nuanced challenges and strategic approaches needed.

Amazon's journey in integrating AI began with identifying precise areas within its colossal operations where AI could make a marked difference. The challenge was immense, given the company's vast array of services and products. Their approach was methodical, employing advanced data analytics and machine learning to understand and predict customer behavior and product demand. This analysis wasn't superficial; it delved deep into customer data, unveiling patterns that would drive strategic AI implementation.

The employees' role in this transformation was pivotal. Amazon integrated AI in ways that augmented, rather than replaced, human tasks. This approach not only improved efficiency but also empowered employees to focus on more strategic, fulfilling roles. AI tools like Alexa were introduced, revolutionizing customer service by reducing the need for constant human intervention, thus exemplifying a harmonious blend of human and artificial intelligence.

Understanding customer perspectives was another area where Amazon excelled. They mastered the art of using AI to deliver personalized customer experiences. This wasn't achieved overnight but through continuous data collection and analysis, leading to AI models that constantly evolved with customer preferences. The result was a significant boost in customer satisfaction and loyalty, a direct outcome of AI-driven personalization.

The technical feasibility of such widespread AI implementation was a complex undertaking. Amazon's approach was collaborative, involving teams across various domains, ensuring that AI initiatives were not only technically sound but also viable and ethically compliant. This meticulous process led to effective AI integration in multiple business areas, from logistics to user experience.

Perhaps the most striking aspect of Amazon's AI journey is the clear demonstration of its return on investment. AI was not just a technological upgrade but a strategic business decision. The company strategically implemented AI in operations where it promised the most significant returns, both in operational efficiency and customer satisfaction. This strategic prioritization and comprehensive cost-benefit analysis underscored the importance of evaluating AI beyond just financial metrics.

Lastly, the selection of tools and techniques for identifying AI opportunities was critical. Amazon's use of a combination of data analytics and machine learning in various business operations exemplified an effective approach in pinpointing areas ripe for AI innovation.

Amazon's story is not just about the successful integration of AI but a narrative that highlights the importance of a strategic, inclusive approach in AI adoption. It serves as an insightful guide for businesses embarking on their AI journey, emphasizing the significance of a holistic, customer-centric approach underpinned by meticulous planning and evaluation.

Conclusion and direct actions for AI Transformation in business

As we culminate our exploration of AI project identification, drawing from Amazon's remarkable journey, let's focus on actionable steps for businesses ready to embark on their AI transformation journey:

1. **Conduct comprehensive business process analysis**: Like Amazon, start with a deep dive into your business processes. Understand and map each step to identify potential areas for AI enhancement.

2. **Engage employees and gather insights**: Implement structured discussions and feedback mechanisms. Employee insights are invaluable in aligning AI integration with practical operational realities.

3. **Prioritize customer centric AI applications**: Systematically gather and analyze customer feedback. Use these insights to

tailor AI solutions that enhance customer experiences and satisfaction.

4. **Assess technical feasibility rigorously**: Collaborate across teams to evaluate the technical feasibility and ethical implications of your AI initiatives. Remember, the goal is to develop AI solutions that are technically sound and ethically compliant.

5. **Articulate a clear business case**: Evaluate the ROI of AI projects, focusing on financial benefits and broader impacts. Prioritize projects that align with strategic business goals and offer tangible benefits.

6. **Select the right tools for AI identification**: Utilize a combination of advanced data analytics, AI readiness assessment tools, and ideation workshops to identify AI opportunities that align with your business objectives.

By following these steps, inspired by Amazon's AI journey, businesses can set a strong foundation for a successful AI transformation. This process emphasizes the importance of strategic planning, stakeholder involvement, and a relentless focus on customer-centricity, aligning perfectly with the Scandinavian ethos of balanced, human-centric technology.

Choosing the right AI project

In the dynamic realm of business technology, artificial intelligence (AI) emerges as a pivotal force of innovation and operational excellence. While our previous discussion, 'Identifying AI projects,' focused on the fundamental aspects of pinpointing AI initiatives within business processes, this chapter, 'Choosing the right AI project,' shifts the lens towards a more strategic viewpoint. We delve into the subtleties of not just identifying, but strategically selecting and executing AI projects that resonate with both business ambitions and the tenets of Scandinavian leadership. This nuanced approach ensures a seamless integration of AI that upholds a balance between technological advancement and human-centric values.

Deepening the understanding of AI applications and projects

To delve deeper into the realm of AI applications and projects, it's essential to recognize the diverse range of possibilities that AI offers. Each business sector can harness AI in unique ways, tailored to its specific challenges and opportunities. For instance, in the healthcare industry, AI can revolutionize patient care through predictive analytics and personalized medicine. In finance, AI can enhance risk assessment and fraud detection, while in retail, it can transform customer experience through personalized recommendations and inventory management.

The selection process for AI projects should be guided by a strategic framework that aligns with the company's long-term vision and immediate operational needs. This involves conducting a thorough analysis of the business processes, identifying areas where AI can bring the most significant impact, and assessing the feasibility of integrating AI solutions into these areas. It's not just about adopting the latest AI technology; it's about finding the right fit for the business's unique ecosystem.

Harvard Business Review [hbr.org] sheds light on the transformative power of AI in project management, underscoring the extensive scope of AI applications across various business functions. This revelation is not just a testament to the versatility of AI but also serves as a beacon, guiding businesses in exploring the myriad ways AI can revolutionize their operations.

TechTarget [techtarget.com] takes this exploration further by detailing 15 top applications of AI in business. This comprehensive list not only emphasizes the expansive role of AI in enhancing business operations but also serves as a valuable resource for businesses seeking to understand how AI can be leveraged in their specific context. From improving customer service with chatbots to optimizing supply chain management through predictive analytics, the applications of AI in business are as diverse as they are impactful.

Deloitte's [deloitte.com] extensive collection of AI use cases across various industries further illuminates the versatility of AI. This compilation is particularly insightful, showcasing how AI can address a wide array of enterprise challenges in innovative ways. Whether it's enhancing marketing strategies with data-driven insights or streamlining HR processes through automation, these use cases provide a rich source of inspiration and practical guidance for businesses looking to embark on their AI journey.

Together, these resources offer a wealth of insights and serve as a roadmap for businesses to select AI projects that not only align with their specific needs but also promise tangible benefits. The key lies in tailoring AI solutions to fit the unique context of each business, ensuring that the chosen AI initiatives are not just technologically advanced but also relevant and impactful.

Tailoring AI to business contexts

Tailoring AI to specific business contexts requires a nuanced approach. It involves understanding the unique characteristics of the business, including its market position, customer base, and internal processes. This understanding enables businesses to identify AI applications that are not only technologically feasible but also strategically aligned with their goals.

For example, an small e-commerce business might benefit more from AI-driven customer service chatbots and targeted marketing algorithms, while a large manufacturing company might find more value in AI-powered predictive maintenance and supply chain optimization. The key is to identify AI applications that complement and enhance the existing strengths of the business while addressing its most pressing challenges.

Identifying and selecting AI applications and projects

The selection of appropriate AI applications and projects is a critical step. This process involves a strategic assessment of the organization's needs, capabilities, and long-term objectives.

- **Needs analysis and strategic alignment**: Begin by analyzing the organization's specific needs and how AI can address them. For example, a logistics company might identify route optimization and inventory management as key areas where AI can bring significant improvements. Align these AI projects with the broader business strategy to ensure they contribute to the overall goals of the organization.

- **Feasibility and impact assessment**: Evaluate the feasibility of proposed AI projects. This includes assessing the technical requirements, data availability, and potential impact on business operations. For instance, a healthcare provider might assess the feasibility of implementing AI for patient data analysis, considering the impact on patient care and operational efficiency.

- **Stakeholder Involvement**: Involve stakeholders, including IT experts, business unit leaders, and potential end-users, in the selection process. Their insights can provide valuable perspectives on the practicality and potential benefits of different AI projects. For example, involving nurses and doctors in the decision-making process for AI tools in a hospital setting can ensure that the selected applications are user-friendly and meet clinical needs.

Implementation strategies and best practices

Once the AI applications and projects are identified, the focus shifts to the nuanced process of implementation. This phase extends beyond the mere technical deployment of AI solutions; it encompasses the holistic integration of these technologies into the existing business ecosystem. A crucial aspect of successful implementation, as suggested by Business Insider [businessinsider.com], is the willingness to challenge traditional norms and adapt to the dynamic capabilities of AI.

The implementation phase should be steered by a set of best practices that align AI solutions with business goals, user needs, and ethical considerations. This includes establishing clear and measurable objectives, actively involving relevant stakeholders in the process, and ensuring transparency and accountability in AI operations. It's about creating a synergy between AI technologies and business processes, ensuring that the AI solutions are not just implemented but are also seamlessly integrated into the fabric of the business.

The selection and implementation of the right AI focus areas are integral to the AI transformation in businesses. By aligning AI initiatives with business objectives and adhering to best practices in implementation and evaluation, organizations can fully unlock the potential of AI. This not only drives innovation and efficiency in their operations but also ensures that AI serves as a catalyst for growth and transformation, resonating with the core values of Scandinavian leadership and human-centric technology.

Best practices in AI implementation

Implementing AI requires a holistic approach that goes beyond technical deployment. It involves preparing the organizational culture for AI adoption, training employees to work alongside AI systems, and establishing robust data governance frameworks.

One best practice is to start small with pilot projects that allow the business to test and learn from AI implementations in a controlled environment. This approach minimizes risk and provides valuable insights that can inform broader AI strategies. Another best practice is to foster a culture of continuous learning and adaptability, ensuring that the workforce is equipped to evolve alongside AI technologies.

Once AI projects are selected, the focus shifts to effective implementation. This stage requires careful planning, resource allocation, and adherence to best practices.

- **Project planning and resource allocation**: Develop a detailed project plan outlining the steps, timelines, and resources required for implementation. Allocate resources efficiently, ensuring that the necessary technology, personnel, and budget are available. For example, a energy company might allocate resources for developing an AI system for predictive maintenance of its infrastructure.

- **Collaboration with AI experts and vendors**: Collaborate with AI experts and vendors to leverage their expertise and ensure the successful implementation of AI projects. For instance, a manufacturing firm might partner with an AI solutions provider to implement advanced machine learning algorithms for quality control.

- **Pilot testing and iterative development**: Start with pilot testing in a controlled environment to identify any issues and make necessary adjustments. Adopt an iterative development approach, allowing for continuous improvement based on feedback and performance metrics. For example, a e-commerce company might pilot an AI-based recommendation system on a small scale before rolling it out across its platform.

Monitoring and evaluating the effectiveness

The journey of AI implementation culminates in the continuous monitoring and evaluation of the effectiveness of the AI projects. This critical step involves setting up robust metrics and KPIs to gauge the impact of AI initiatives on business performance. Forbes [forbes.com] highlights the increasing reliance of businesses on AI to enhance their operations, underscoring the importance of ongoing assessment and refinement of AI strategies.

Regular evaluation is key to identifying areas for improvement and ensuring that AI projects remain aligned with the evolving needs of the business and advancements in technology. This process not only provides valuable insights into the ROI of AI initiatives but also aids businesses in making informed decisions about future investments in AI.

- **Performance metrics and KPIs**: Establish clear performance metrics and key performance indicators (KPIs) to measure the success of AI projects. These metrics should align with the objectives of the AI initiatives and the overall business goals. For example, a marketing agency might measure the success of its AI-driven customer segmentation project by tracking engagement rates and conversion metrics.

- **Regular reviews and adjustments**: Conduct regular reviews of AI projects to assess their performance and make necessary adjustments. This includes analyzing the data generated by AI systems, gathering feedback from users, and comparing the outcomes with the set objectives. For example, a retail chain might regularly review the performance of its AI-powered inventory management system to ensure it meets the demand forecasting accuracy.

- **Long-term evaluation and scalability**: Evaluate the long-term impact of AI projects on business operations and scalability. Consider how these projects can be scaled up or adapted to meet evolving business needs. For instance, a financial institution might assess the scalability of its AI-driven fraud detection system as transaction volumes grow.

In wrapping up "Choosing the right AI project," it's essential to crystallize the chapter's essence into actionable insights. The journey of integrating AI into your business isn't just about embracing new technology; it's a strategic endeavor that should resonate with your company's long-term vision and present requirements. The art lies in customizing AI to fit the unique tapestry of your organization, understanding its nuances, market position, and specific needs. It's about a methodical selection process, underpinned by an informed understanding of your business landscape and a collaborative approach to involve key stakeholders. Implementation should be carried out with a keen eye on adaptability and learning, ensuring pilot projects pave the way for broader strategies. And, the cycle of AI integration doesn't end with deployment; it demands ongoing evaluation and adaptation, ensuring these advanced tools evolve alongside your business. This holistic approach ensures AI becomes a true catalyst for innovation and growth, harmonizing with the core values of Scandinavian leadership and human-centric technology.

Prioritize AI transformation

In the transformative journey towards AI integration, the decision-making process for allocating resources is a critical strategic endeavor. This process involves a comprehensive evaluation of where to channel investments – whether in technology, talent, or data infrastructure – to effectively harness AI's transformative power.

Strategic resource assessment: The initial step is a strategic assessment of the current resource landscape. This encompasses an evaluation of the existing technological infrastructure, the skill level of employees, and the quality and readiness of available data. For instance, a manufacturing firm might find that while their machinery is state-of-the-art, their data management systems are not optimized for AI integration. This assessment lays the groundwork for informed decision-making.

Resource allocation framework: Developing a robust framework for resource allocation is crucial. This framework should balance the immediate needs for AI implementation with the organization's long-term strategic objectives. An e-commerce company, for example, might allocate more resources towards developing AI-driven customer analytics, foreseeing its significant long-term impact on customer satisfaction and retention.

Cost-Benefit analysis: A thorough cost-benefit analysis is essential for each potential investment area. This analysis should extend beyond immediate financial implications to consider factors like scalability, adaptability, and potential ROI in terms of efficiency, innovation, and market competitiveness. For example, a logistics company might evaluate the costs of integrating AI in warehouse management against the expected efficiency gains and the long-term benefits of improved supply chain management.

Stakeholder engagement and collaboration: Involving key stakeholders in the resource allocation decision-making process is vital. This includes not just the C-suite executives but also IT leaders, data scientists, and representatives from departments that will be directly impacted by AI integration. Their insights and perspectives provide a more comprehensive understanding of where resources are most critically needed. For instance, input from frontline employees in a retail chain might highlight areas where AI can significantly improve customer service or inventory management.

Prioritization of AI initiatives: Prioritizing AI initiatives based on their alignment with business goals and potential impact is a key aspect of resource allocation. This involves identifying AI projects that will most effectively drive the company towards achieving its strategic objectives, such as market expansion, customer engagement, or operational efficiency. It is not enough to have an AI transformation as wish, you need to allocate both human resources to anchor the project in the operation and allocate capital as the initial investment is not free and it will take time for the investment to pay off. So, the notion of a "free" investment should be forgotten.

Monitoring and adjusting resource allocation: Continuous monitoring of the effectiveness of resource allocation towards AI initiatives is crucial. This allows for adjustments and reallocations as needed, ensuring that resources are being utilized in the most impactful way. Regular reviews and assessments can help a financial institution, for instance, to fine-tune its investment in AI-driven risk assessment tools, ensuring they remain aligned with evolving market conditions and regulatory requirements. The best idea is to install standardized KPI for the project in your business database and as an initial AI project include a simple AI function which monitors the AI project and gives feedback and guidance. This will both be a fun initial project for the project owners and a validation of the utilization of AI in business processes.

Balancing short-term needs and long-term vision: Balancing the immediate needs of AI projects with the long-term vision of the company is essential. This balance ensures that resource allocation not only addresses current challenges but also sets the foundation for future growth and innovation. A hospitality company, for instance, might invest in AI for immediate operational improvements while also considering future applications of AI in enhancing guest experiences.

Risk assessment and mitigation: Assessing and mitigating risks associated with AI projects is an integral part of the resource allocation process. This includes evaluating risks related to technology adoption, data security, and compliance with regulations. An automotive manufacturer, for example, might assess the risks involved in implementing AI in autonomous vehicle systems, ensuring that safety and regulatory standards are rigorously met.

By meticulously navigating the decision processes for allocating resources to AI, businesses can strategically position themselves to leverage AI's capabilities effectively. This approach not only fosters innovation and efficiency but also aligns with the organization's broader strategic goals, ensuring a sustainable and impactful AI transformation journey.

Identifying and phasing out outdated processes or technologies

In the dynamic landscape of AI transformation, identifying and methodically phasing out outdated processes, technologies, and legacy systems are not just a necessity but a strategic imperative. This step is crucial for maintaining a competitive edge and operational efficiency in the rapidly evolving digital era. You can include this as a general upgrade of the company's platform if you wish. To take an analogy from a completely different area; you would not build a new self-driving electrical car on the chassis of a Lada from the 1970's. If you want the best results, you also need internal systems which can effectively communicate with an AI without latency and errors.

Audit of existing processes and technologies: The first step involves a thorough audit of current business processes, technologies, and systems. This audit aims to pinpoint areas where AI can significantly enhance efficiency or where existing methods are becoming obsolete. For instance, a financial institution might discover that their traditional risk assessment models are less effective compared to AI-driven predictive models. This realization is the catalyst for change, prompting a strategic re-evaluation of current methodologies. But do not get blindsided by mere data and documentation, the biggest effects of an AI system can easily be found where there is no current documentation. It could be as easy as an automated curation of links and automation in a browser toolbar which could save the office employees huge amount of time if they daily uses large amount of time consolidating and communicating across many tools.

Development of a phasing out plan: Once outdated processes and systems are identified, the next step is to develop a structured plan for their gradual elimination. This plan should carefully consider the impact on current operations and establish a clear timeline for the transition to more AI-centric processes. For example, a healthcare provider might devise a plan for a gradual shift from manual patient record-keeping to an AI-powered digital system, ensuring minimal disruption to patient care during the transition.

Change management and employee training: Effective change management strategies are essential to facilitate this transition. This includes comprehensive training programs for employees to adapt to new technologies, a phased implementation approach for introducing AI solutions, and continuous monitoring of the impact on business operations. For instance, a hotel chain might introduce an AI-based booking system in stages, providing ample training and support to staff to ensure a smooth adaptation to the new technology.

Integration with existing systems: A critical aspect of this process is the integration of new AI technologies with existing legacy systems. This step ensures continuity and prevents operational disruptions. A manufacturing company, for instance, might explore ways to integrate AI-driven predictive maintenance tools with their existing machinery control systems, ensuring seamless operation during the transition.

Stakeholder communication and involvement: Keeping all stakeholders, including employees, customers, suppliers, and partners, informed and involved in the phasing-out process is vital. This approach fosters a sense of inclusivity and transparency. For example, a retail company might communicate with its suppliers about the shift to an AI-driven inventory management system, explaining the benefits and changes in the supply chain process.

Evaluation of cost implications: Assessing the cost implications of phasing out outdated processes is a key consideration. This includes evaluating the cost of new AI technologies against the expected efficiency gains and potential for revenue growth. A logistics company, for instance, might weigh the costs of integrating AI in warehouse management against the anticipated improvements in operational efficiency.

Monitoring and feedback mechanisms: Establishing robust monitoring and feedback mechanisms is essential to evaluate the effectiveness of new AI-driven processes and make necessary adjustments. For instance, a healthcare provider might implement patient outcome tracking and staff feedback mechanisms after transitioning to an AI-powered digital record-keeping system.

Legal and compliance considerations: Ensuring compliance with legal and regulatory standards during the transition is crucial. For example, a manufacturing company must ensure that the integration of AI-driven tools with their machinery control systems adheres to industry safety standards and regulations.

Sustainability and environmental impact: Considering the environmental impact of phasing out old technologies and processes is particularly important for companies committed to sustainability. For example, a hotel chain might evaluate the environmental benefits of an AI-based booking system, such as reduced paper usage and energy-efficient data management.

By methodically identifying and phasing out outdated processes and technologies, businesses can strategically embrace AI transformation, ensuring that their operations are not only more efficient and competitive but also aligned with their long-term goals and values. This approach is fundamental to thriving in the age of digital transformation and AI integration.

Challenges of transformation and how to address them

Transforming an organization to integrate AI involves navigating a complex landscape of challenges. These challenges are not just technical but also cultural, operational, and strategic. Addressing these effectively is crucial for a successful AI transformation.

Technical challenges

Compatibility with existing IT infrastructure: One of the primary technical challenges is ensuring that new AI technologies seamlessly integrate with existing IT systems. This requires a detailed assessment of current infrastructure and possibly upgrading or adapting it to support AI functionalities. For example, a telecom company might need to upgrade its network infrastructure to support AI-driven data analytics and customer service solutions.

Data privacy and security: With the increasing emphasis on data-driven decision-making, ensuring data privacy and adhering to regulations like GDPR becomes paramount. Implementing robust data security measures and privacy protocols is essential. This might involve encrypting data, implementing access controls, and regularly auditing data usage.

Reliability and accuracy of AI systems: Ensuring the reliability of AI systems is critical. This involves not only the accuracy of AI algorithms but also their consistency and predictability. Regular testing, validation, and updating of AI models are necessary to maintain their reliability. For instance, an AI model used in healthcare for patient diagnosis must undergo rigorous testing to ensure its accuracy and reliability.

Cultural resistance

Education and communication: Overcoming cultural resistance is often about changing mindsets and attitudes towards AI. This can be achieved through comprehensive education and communication strategies. For instance, a design firm might implement a series of workshops and seminars to familiarize their creative team with AI tools, showcasing how AI can enhance their creative processes rather than replace them.

Creating AI advocates: Encouraging a culture where employees become AI advocates can significantly reduce resistance. This involves identifying and training key personnel who can champion AI initiatives within the organization and help their colleagues understand the benefits and opportunities AI brings.

Addressing fear of job displacement: One of the common cultural resistances to AI is the fear of job displacement. Addressing this fear transparently, showing how AI can augment rather than replace human roles, and providing retraining and upskilling opportunities are essential steps.

Continuous learning and adaptation

Staying abreast of AI advancements: AI is a rapidly evolving field. Organizations must stay updated with the latest developments and be ready to adapt their strategies accordingly. For instance, a marketing agency might regularly update its AI algorithms to keep up with the latest trends in consumer behavior analysis, ensuring they remain competitive and effective.

Building a learning organization: Cultivating a learning organization where continuous skill development and knowledge sharing are encouraged is vital. This includes regular training sessions, attending AI conferences and workshops, and subscribing to relevant AI research and publications.

Feedback loops and iterative improvement: Establishing feedback mechanisms where employees can share their experiences and challenges with AI tools helps in continuous improvement. Iterative development based on this feedback ensures that AI solutions are aligned with user needs and organizational goals.

Addressing the challenges of AI transformation requires a multifaceted approach, encompassing technical, cultural, strategic, and operational aspects. By acknowledging and strategically tackling these challenges, organizations can successfully navigate the journey of AI integration, reaping its benefits while minimizing disruptions and resistance.

In conclusion, prioritization and exclusion in AI transformation are about making strategic decisions that align with the company's long-term vision. It's a balancing act between adopting new technologies, phasing out the old, and managing the transformation journey effectively. By addressing these aspects thoughtfully, businesses can navigate the AI landscape successfully, ensuring that their journey in AI transformation is both progressive and sustainable.

Preparing AI-ready data

In the realm of AI, the adage "garbage in, garbage out" is not just a cliché but a stark reality. The quality and accessibility of data are the bedrock upon which effective AI systems are built. High-quality data ensures that AI models are fed with accurate, relevant, and comprehensive information, leading to more reliable and effective outcomes. This is crucial in fostering trust among users and stakeholders, especially in a business environment where decisions based on AI can have significant implications.

For instance, a study highlighted by SnapLogic [snaplogic.com] reveals the impact of poor data quality in AI, underscoring how it directly affects the performance, accuracy, and reliability of AI models. Similarly, Forbes [forbes.com] emphasizes that data quality is a major bottleneck in AI adoption, suggesting that overcoming this challenge is key to harnessing the full potential of AI technologies.

What does 'AI-Ready' data mean?

AI-ready data refers to datasets that are structured, organized, and cleansed, making them effectively usable by AI algorithms. Such data must be free from inconsistencies, gaps, and errors, and presented in a format easily processed by AI systems.

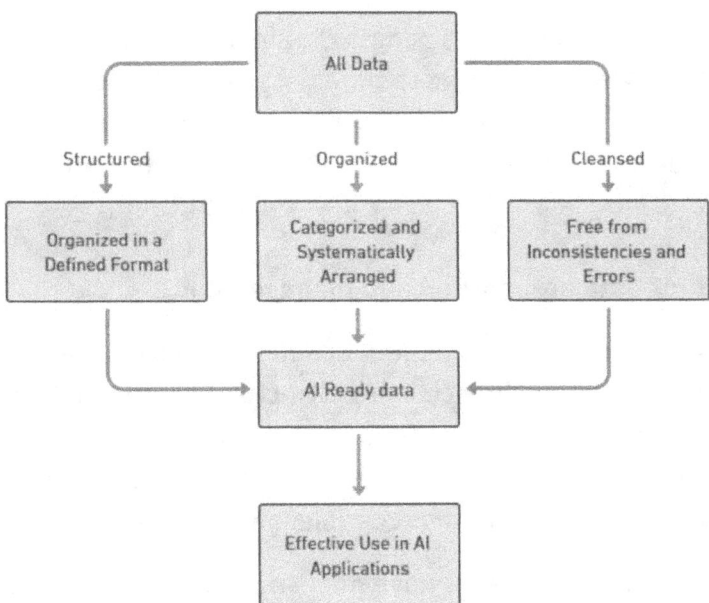

The journey into the AI landscape for businesses begins with a thorough assessment of the existing datasets to determine their suitability for AI applications. This process involves an in-depth evaluation of various aspects of the data crucial for their usability in AI systems.

1. **Data quality**: This includes examining whether the existing data are accurate and consistent. Accuracy ensures that the data accurately reflect the real world, crucial for making reliable decisions based on AI analysis. Consistency is equally

important, as inconsistent data can lead to confusing results and unreliable conclusions when processed by AI algorithms.

2. **Data completeness**: Ensuring no missing values or gaps in datasets is critical. Missing data can result in AI systems deriving incorrect patterns or missing key insights, crucial for accurate analyses.

3. **Data format**: The format of data is a significant factor to consider. AI systems often require data in specific formats to process them effectively. This may involve evaluating whether the existing data are structured or unstructured.

Methods for data preparation and management

Data preparation and management are critical steps in making data AI-ready. This involves cleaning, structuring, and enriching data to ensure it is in a format that AI systems can effectively process and analyze. It's not just about having data; it's about having data that is organized, accessible, and meaningful.

Technological advancements have made data preparation more efficient and effective. Tools and platforms are available that automate many aspects of data preparation, reducing the time and effort required while increasing accuracy. For example, AI-driven data preparation tools can automatically detect and correct errors, fill in missing values, and identify outliers.

Improving data for AI integration

In preparing data for AI integration, businesses face several key tasks to ensure their data are optimally aligned for effective use in AI systems.

Data cleansing: The first and foremost step in preparing data for AI integration is data cleansing. This process involves meticulously identifying and correcting errors and inconsistencies in the data. Common issues include duplicate entries, missing values, and incorrect data entries. For instance, in a customer database, data cleansing would involve rectifying misspelled names, standardizing address formats, and filling in missing contact details. This step is crucial because even minor errors can significantly skew AI model outcomes, leading to unreliable predictions or insights.

Data structuring: Many AI models require data to be in a structured format for efficient processing and analysis. This step is particularly challenging when dealing with unstructured data, such as text, images, or videos. Data structuring involves organizing this data into a more systematic format, like databases or spreadsheets. Techniques such as Natural Language Processing (NLP) for text data, image tagging for visual data, and audio transcription for sound files are employed to convert unstructured data into a structured form. For example, converting customer feedback from various social media platforms into a structured format for sentiment analysis.

Data enrichment: This involves augmenting existing datasets with additional, relevant information to make them more comprehensive for AI analysis. Data enrichment can significantly enhance the quality of insights derived from AI models. For instance, in a sales dataset, adding information about weather conditions or local events can help in understanding the external factors influencing sales trends. Data enrichment not only adds depth to the analysis but also aids in uncovering hidden correlations and patterns that would otherwise go unnoticed.

Standardization and normalization: Ensuring consistency across the dataset is essential for AI models to function correctly. Standardization involves bringing different data formats into a uniform format, while normalization adjusts the range of data values for better comparability. For example, standardizing date formats across a global sales dataset or normalizing prices to a single currency.

Data integration: Often, valuable data is spread across various sources and systems within an organization. Integrating these disparate data sources into a single, cohesive dataset is crucial for comprehensive AI analysis. This might involve merging databases, aligning data fields, and ensuring seamless data flow between systems.

Quality assurance and validation: After data cleansing, structuring, enrichment, standardization, and integration, it's vital to perform quality assurance checks. This step ensures that the data is not only clean and well-structured but also relevant and reliable for the intended AI application. Validation techniques, such as cross-referencing with external data sources or running sample analyses, help in verifying the accuracy and applicability of the data.

By meticulously executing these steps, businesses can transform their raw data into a valuable asset for AI applications. This transformation not only facilitates more accurate and insightful AI analyses but also positions the organization to leverage AI for strategic decision-making and innovation.

Drawing a line in the sand: Deciding when to discard old data

A critical decision in managing data for AI is determining when to discard old data in favor of new. This involves weighing the cost benefits and relevance of the data. Old data might provide historical insights, but it may not be as relevant for current models. Conversely, focusing solely on new data might miss out on valuable trends and patterns evident in historical data. The key is to strike a balance, ensuring that the data used is both representative and relevant.

Technological advances in data preparation

The landscape of data preparation has been revolutionized by technological advances. Tools like Talend, Informatica, and Trifacta leverage AI and machine learning to streamline the data preparation process. These tools can automate data cleaning, integration, and transformation processes, making it easier for businesses to prepare large datasets for AI applications.

For example, Talend's Data Fabric offers a suite of apps that simplify data integration, ensuring that data is clean, complete, and compliant. This kind of technology not only saves time but also enhances the accuracy and reliability of data used in AI models.

Integrating and updating current data structures for AI

Integrating and updating current data structures for AI readiness is a complex but essential task. It involves ensuring that existing data systems are compatible with AI technologies and can handle the scale and complexity of AI-driven processes. This might require updating legacy systems, adopting new data storage solutions, or implementing data governance practices to ensure data quality and accessibility.

Success metrics and ROI

Measuring the success of AI initiatives and their return on investment (ROI) is crucial for businesses. Success metrics might include improved efficiency, increased revenue, cost savings, or enhanced customer satisfaction. For instance, a retail company implemented an AI-driven inventory management system, resulting in a 20% reduction in inventory costs and a 10% increase in sales due to better stock availability.

Considerations around data ethics and compliance

Data ethics and compliance are increasingly important in the AI landscape. This involves ensuring that data is used responsibly, respecting privacy, and adhering to regulatory requirements. For example, GDPR in the EU has set a new standard for data privacy, requiring businesses to be more transparent about how they collect, use, and protect data.

Preparing AI-ready data is a multifaceted process that requires attention to quality, management, technological advancements, and ethical considerations. By focusing on these aspects, businesses can ensure that their AI initiatives are built on a solid foundation of reliable and effective data.

Challenges of using Non-AI-Ready data

Using non-AI-ready data in AI systems presents significant challenges that can compromise the effectiveness and value of AI initiatives.

Low precision in AI predictions: The accuracy of AI models is heavily dependent on the quality of the data they are trained with. When data is riddled with errors, inconsistencies, or gaps, AI systems face significant challenges in accurately identifying patterns and trends. This can lead to unreliable predictions and analyses, which can be detrimental in critical decision-making scenarios. For example, in a financial forecasting model, if the input data is inaccurate or inconsistent, the AI might predict incorrect market trends, leading to poor investment decisions.

Longer training time for AI models: The process of cleaning and preparing data for AI systems is not only meticulous but also time-intensive. When starting with non-AI-ready data, significant effort is required to identify and correct errors, fill gaps, and ensure consistency. This extended preprocessing phase delays the development and deployment of AI models, postponing the realization of their benefits. In sectors like healthcare, where timely data analysis is crucial for patient care, delays in model training can hinder the timely implementation of AI-driven diagnostic tools.

Increased costs for data maintenance and cleaning: Transforming non-AI-ready data into a usable format for AI applications involves substantial investment in both labor and technology. This includes costs associated with data cleaning tools, data scientists' time, and potentially, third-party services for data processing. These expenses can be particularly burdensome for small to medium-sized enterprises (SMEs) with limited budgets. For instance, a small e-commerce business might find the cost of converting historical sales data into an AI-compatible format prohibitively expensive, impacting its ability to leverage AI for personalized customer recommendations.

Risk of data misinterpretation: Non-AI-ready data, due to its inherent flaws, poses a risk of misinterpretation by AI systems. AI models might draw incorrect conclusions or overlook critical insights due to incomplete or inconsistent data. This can lead to misguided business strategies or operational inefficiencies. For example, a logistics company using flawed data for route optimization might end up with inefficient routing, leading to increased fuel costs and delivery delays.

Compliance and ethical concerns: In the age of stringent data privacy regulations, using non-AI-ready data can lead to compliance issues, especially if the data contains inaccuracies or outdated information. Moreover, ethical concerns arise when AI models trained on poor-quality data make decisions that affect individuals' lives, such as in law enforcement or credit scoring.

To address these challenges, businesses must prioritize the preparation of AI-ready data. This involves not only technical processes of data cleaning and structuring but also strategic decision-making about data sources and management practices. By ensuring their data is AI-ready, businesses can fully harness the power of AI, driving innovation and maintaining a competitive edge in the digital era.

This insight is crucial for companies, as it underscores the importance of data quality and preparation in AI projects. Ensuring that data are AI-ready is not just a technical necessity but a strategic investment in the future success of the business.

Education and cultural change

The journey towards AI transformation in an organization is deeply rooted in education. A comprehensive AI education program is not just about imparting technical knowledge; it's a strategic initiative to cultivate an AI-centric mindset throughout the organization. Each employee needs to see a reason for playing around with the new technology, trying out new areas and innovate both for personal and professional usage.

Holistic curriculum design: Develop a curriculum that covers a broad spectrum of AI topics. This should include foundational AI concepts, ethical considerations, and industry-specific applications. Do not limit yourself with topics only centring around the core business topics, give also education and guidance about what the possibilities of AI can be, e.g. use it to create dinner recipes based on what is left in the fridge tonight, as employees might get inspired and create ground breaking innovation by exploring farfetched use cases.

Role-specific customization: Design customized learning pathways tailored to different roles within the organization. Technical staff require in-depth training in AI algorithms and data science. Conversely, sales and marketing teams need to understand how AI can enhance customer engagement and predictive analytics. This approach ensures that each department harnesses AI's potential relevant to their functions.

Collaborative learning platforms: Establish partnerships with academic institutions or leverage online learning platforms to offer cutting-edge AI courses. For example, an enterprise might collaborate with the local University, blending academic research with real-world business applications. This partnership could involve guest lectures, joint research projects, and internships for students. While a SME might utilize LinkedIn learning and other generic platform to give a broader understanding for the teams.

Incentivized learning programs: Encourage participation in AI education through incentives. Implement a recognition system where employees earn certifications upon course completion. Link these achievements to career advancement opportunities, such as eligibility for specific projects or promotions. This system not only motivates employees but also helps in building a skilled workforce ready to tackle AI challenges.

Interactive and engaging learning methods: Utilize interactive learning methods such as gamification, simulations, and real-world project assignments. These methods make learning more engaging and effective.

Continuous learning and development: AI is a rapidly evolving field. Establish a culture of continuous learning where employees are encouraged to regularly update their AI knowledge. This could be facilitated through recurrent refresher courses, subscriptions to AI journals, or access to online resources.

Feedback-driven improvement: Regularly gather feedback from participants to continuously improve the AI education program. This feedback should inform the curriculum's relevance, teaching methods, and overall effectiveness.

Developing an AI education program is a strategic imperative for organizations embarking on AI transformation. By creating customized, collaborative, and incentivized learning pathways, and fostering a culture of continuous development and feedback, organizations can effectively prepare their workforce for the AI-driven future. This approach not only equips employees with necessary AI skills but also embeds a culture of innovation and adaptability essential for thriving in the digital era.

Promoting a culture supporting AI and continuous learning

The successful integration of AI into business processes hinges on cultivating a culture that not only embraces AI but also values continuous learning and innovation. This cultural shift is pivotal for organizations to fully leverage AI's potential.

Leadership as AI Champions: Leadership plays a crucial role in shaping organizational culture. Leaders should not only endorse AI initiatives but also actively engage in AI learning programs. For example, executives in a firm could participate in AI workshops, sharing their insights and learnings with the wider team. This visible commitment can significantly influence the organization's attitude towards AI adoption.

Building AI learning communities: Establish internal AI learning communities or forums where employees can share knowledge, discuss AI trends, and brainstorm applications. These communities should be cross-functional, encouraging diverse perspectives and collaborative problem-solving. For instance, a company could set up an AI innovation hub where employees from different departments collaborate on AI projects, sharing insights and learning from each other.

Promoting a Safe-to-Fail environment: Encourage a culture where experimentation with AI is not just allowed but celebrated, even when it doesn't always lead to immediate success. This approach fosters innovation and helps in discovering novel AI applications. For example, a company could implement a 'fail fast, learn fast' policy, where teams are encouraged to test new AI-driven models, learn from the outcomes, and iterate rapidly.

Recognition and reward systems: Implement recognition and reward systems that acknowledge and celebrate AI-driven innovations and learning achievements. This could include awards for the best AI project of the year or recognition for employees who have significantly upskilled in AI. Such initiatives motivate employees to engage more deeply with AI technologies.

Integrating AI into corporate values: Embed AI and continuous learning into the core values of the organization. This integration can be reflected in mission statements, corporate communications, and strategic objectives. For instance, a company could include 'embracing digital innovation' as one of its core values, reflecting its commitment to AI and technology-driven growth.

Regular AI updates and communications: Keep the workforce informed about AI developments within the organization and the industry. Regular newsletters, seminars, and webinars on AI topics can keep the excitement and conversation around AI alive. For example, a retail company could host monthly AI talks featuring internal or external AI experts discussing the latest trends and applications in retail.

Promoting a culture that supports AI and continuous learning is a multifaceted endeavour. It requires leadership commitment, the creation of collaborative learning environments, a culture that encourages experimentation, and the integration of AI into the organizational ethos. By fostering such a culture, businesses can not only smoothly integrate AI into their operations but also continually innovate and stay ahead in the rapidly evolving digital landscape.

Leadership and employee engagement in AI changes

The transition to AI-driven operations necessitates not just technological adaptation but also a strong alignment between leadership and the workforce. Effective leadership and active employee engagement are key to successfully navigating the complexities of AI transformation.

Transparent and continuous communication: Leadership must prioritize clear and ongoing communication about AI initiatives. This involves articulating the objectives, potential benefits, and expected changes brought by AI. For instance, a manufacturing company's leadership could regularly update employees on how AI will enhance production efficiency, explaining the tangible benefits and addressing any concerns. This transparency helps in building trust and aligning everyone towards common goals.

Inclusive participation in AI projects: Encourage employee involvement in AI projects right from the conceptual stage. This participatory approach not only fosters a sense of ownership among employees but also leverages their insights for more effective AI solutions. For example, a healthcare provider could involve medical staff in developing AI tools for patient care, ensuring that the tools are practical and user-friendly.

Feedback loops and adaptation: Implement feedback mechanisms that allow employees to voice their opinions and concerns about AI implementations. Regularly assess and refine AI strategies based on this feedback. This approach ensures that AI initiatives are in sync with both employee needs and business objectives. For instance, a logistics firm could use surveys and focus groups to gather employee feedback on an AI-based inventory management system, making adjustments based on their input.

Leadership training in AI competency: Equip leaders with the necessary AI knowledge and skills. This training enables them to lead AI projects effectively and make informed decisions. For instance, a finance company could provide its executives with training in AI applications in financial analytics, preparing them to lead AI integration in their departments.

Recognition of AI contributions: Acknowledge and reward employees who actively contribute to AI projects or show significant progress in AI-related skills. This recognition can be in the form of awards, promotions, or public acknowledgment. For example, a retail chain might institute an 'AI Innovator of the Month' award to celebrate employees who come up with innovative AI applications in customer service.

Building AI advocates within the workforce: Identify and nurture AI advocates or champions within the organization. These are employees who are enthusiastic about AI and can influence their peers positively. For example, a marketing firm could empower tech-savvy marketers to share their AI project successes and learning experiences with their teams.

Balancing human and AI roles: Leadership should clearly define the roles of AI and human employees, emphasizing how AI complements rather than replaces human skills. For example, a shipping company could demonstrate how AI enhances decision-making in navigation, while the crew's expertise remains invaluable.

Leadership and employee engagement in AI changes are about creating a collaborative ecosystem where AI is seen as a tool for enhancement rather than a threat. It requires transparent communication, inclusive participation, continuous feedback, and a clear understanding of the evolving roles in an AI-integrated workplace. By fostering this synergy, organizations can smoothly transition into AI-enhanced operations, ensuring both employee satisfaction and business efficiency.

Transitioning to AI integration is a multifaceted journey encompassing technological, educational, and cultural shifts. By developing comprehensive AI education programs, fostering a culture supportive of AI and continuous learning, and ensuring robust leadership and employee engagement, organizations can effectively navigate this transformation. This approach not only prepares the workforce for an AI-driven future but also cultivates an environment where AI is viewed as an integral tool for innovation and growth.

The future of AI in business

In an era where digital transformation is not just a trend but a necessity, the role of artificial intelligence (AI) in shaping the future of business is both exciting and pivotal. As we embark on this journey through the labyrinth of AI's potential, it's crucial to understand its trajectory and implications. This chapter delves into the evolving landscape of AI, offering insights into its future trends and roles in business, and concludes with practical advice for embracing these changes.

As we predict the future of AI in business, remember, it's a field where today's 'cutting-edge' is tomorrow's 'remember when we thought that was cool?

Now I will do a dangerous and potential stupid move and try to do predictions and foresee trends within AI and Its role in future business, although it is moving so fast so these might have been changed before this book is even published.

1. **Generative AI**: The democratization of AI is on the horizon. Generative AI, known for creating content, is becoming more accessible. This trend signifies a shift towards AI as a tool for creativity and innovation, opening new avenues for business applications.

2. **Multimodal AI**: The future beckons a more integrated approach to AI. Multimodal AI, which processes diverse data types like text, images, and sound, is set to revolutionize how businesses understand and interact with their data. This advancement isn't just about technology; it's about creating systems that understand the world more like humans do.

3. **AI in decision making**: AI's role in strategic decision-making is becoming more pronounced. With its ability to analyze vast datasets and predict trends, AI is becoming an indispensable tool for business leaders, offering insights that drive smarter, data-driven decisions.

4. **Ethical AI and regulation**: As AI becomes more prevalent, the focus on ethical AI and regulation will intensify. Businesses will need to navigate the complexities of using AI responsibly, ensuring compliance with evolving regulations and ethical standards.

5. **AI and employee interaction**: The interaction between AI and employees will evolve. AI will not only augment employee capabilities but also require new skill sets. This shift necessitates a focus on training and development, ensuring that employees are equipped to work alongside AI effectively.

6. **Economic impact**: AI's contribution to the economy is staggering. By 2030, it's projected to boost the United States GDP by 21%. This trend is a global phenomenon, indicating AI's role as a key driver in economic growth and business efficiency.

Final considerations and advice for readers

As we look towards the future, it's clear that AI will continue to be a transformative force in business. However, embracing AI is not just about adopting new technologies; it's about adapting to a new way of thinking and operating. Businesses must be willing to experiment, learn from failures, and continuously adapt. It's about fostering a culture that embraces change and innovation.

For leaders, the challenge is to **think big but start small**. Begin by identifying specific areas where AI can add value, and gradually expand its role across the organization. It's also crucial to invest in your people, equipping them with the skills and knowledge to work effectively with AI.

In conclusion, the future of AI in business is not just about technological advancement; it's about how we integrate this technology into our organizations in a way that is ethical, responsible, and human-centric. By doing so, we can harness the full potential of AI to drive innovation, efficiency, and growth.

New trends and challenges in AI

As we navigate the uncharted waters of the AI revolution, it's imperative to stay abreast of the latest trends and challenges. This chapter offers a deep dive into the evolving landscape of AI, exploring how these advancements are shaping the future of business and society. From personalization to ethical dilemmas, we'll explore the multifaceted nature of AI's growth and its implications.

Transformative AI in business

Personalization: AI is increasingly tailoring experiences to individual preferences, transforming how businesses interact with customers. From customized product recommendations to personalized marketing strategies, AI's ability to analyze consumer behavior is revolutionizing customer engagement.

Microinteractions: AI is enhancing user experience through subtle but impactful microinteractions. These small, automated responses in digital interfaces are making technology more intuitive and user-friendly, significantly improving customer satisfaction.

Accessibility: AI is breaking down barriers, making technology more accessible to diverse populations. From voice recognition software that aids those with disabilities to translation services that bridge language gaps, AI is democratizing access to information and services.

Multitasking robots: The development of AI-powered robots capable of performing multiple tasks is transforming industries. From manufacturing to healthcare, these robots are increasing efficiency and productivity, but also reshaping the workforce.

AI talent and customization

Customized AI models: Businesses are increasingly adopting AI models tailored to their specific needs. This customization allows for more precise and effective solutions, driving innovation and efficiency.

Talent needs: The rise of AI is creating a demand for new skill sets. There's a growing need for AI specialists who can develop and manage these customized models, as well as for employees who can work effectively alongside AI.

Risks and moral dilemmas

Shadow AI: The proliferation of unauthorized AI applications within organizations, known as Shadow AI, poses significant risks. These include security vulnerabilities and compliance issues, necessitating stricter governance and oversight.

Ethical challenges: As AI becomes more pervasive, ethical considerations are coming to the forefront. Issues like bias in AI algorithms and the ethical use of AI-generated data are critical concerns that businesses must address.

Creativity and integrity

AI in creative industries: AI is making inroads into creative fields, from music production to content creation. This trend is opening up new possibilities for innovation but also raises questions about originality and intellectual property.

Disinformation challenges: The ability of AI to generate realistic fake content is a growing concern. Businesses must be vigilant against the spread of disinformation and invest in AI that can detect and counteract these threats.

The landscape of AI is dynamic and complex, filled with exciting opportunities and significant challenges. As we embrace these new trends, it's crucial to do so with a mindful approach, considering the ethical, societal, and business implications. The future of AI is not just about technological advancement; it's about shaping a future that aligns with our values and aspirations.

In an AI-transformed world, the only constant is change, and it's digitally brilliant.

Case studies and success stories

In the journey of AI transformation, real-world examples serve as invaluable guides. This chapter delves into two compelling case studies: Universal Robots and ElevenLabs. These stories are not just narratives of technological innovation; they are testaments to the seamless integration of AI in enhancing human capabilities and addressing market needs. Chosen for their relevance and impact, these cases perfectly embody the core themes of this book – leveraging AI to foster collaboration, innovation, and human-centric solutions in the business world. As we explore their journeys, we uncover practical insights and strategies that resonate with our overarching goal: ensuring human priorities in the age of automation. These cases are chosen for their alignment with the Scandinavian leadership philosophy, emphasizing egalitarianism, employee well-being, and a balanced approach to technology – principles that are increasingly vital in today's AI-driven business landscape.

Universal Robots: Revolutionizing manufacturing with AI-enhanced robots

Source: The European Business Review - Universal Robots

Situation before AI integration: Prior to embracing AI, Universal Robots, like many in the manufacturing sector, relied on traditional robotic solutions that were less flexible and required significant programming and maintenance. These limitations posed challenges in adapting to varied and intricate manufacturing tasks.

Vision for AI integration: Universal Robots envisioned creating a new class of robots that could work alongside humans, enhancing productivity and flexibility in manufacturing processes. Their goal was to develop robots that were easy to program, adaptable, and could safely interact with human workers.

AI strategy: The company's strategy involved integrating AI to make robots more intuitive and capable of learning from their environment. This included using AI algorithms for machine learning, computer vision, and advanced sensor technology, enabling robots to perform complex tasks with high precision.

Impact on productivity and competitiveness: The AI-enhanced robots led to a transformative impact on productivity, with over 50% improvement in manufacturing efficiency. This leap in productivity positioned Universal Robots as a leader in the robot market, significantly enhancing their competitiveness in the global manufacturing industry.

AI tools used: Universal Robots utilized a range of AI tools, including machine learning algorithms for adaptive learning and computer vision systems for precise object recognition and manipulation. These tools allowed their robots to understand and adapt to different manufacturing environments, making them versatile and efficient.

ElevenLabs: Pioneering AI in Voice Synthesis

Source: Euronews - ElevenLabs

Situation before AI integration: Before venturing into AI, the voice synthesis market was dominated by basic text-to-speech technologies that lacked realism and customization. ElevenLabs identified a gap in the market for more natural and versatile voice synthesis solutions.

Vision for AI integration: ElevenLabs aimed to revolutionize the voice synthesis industry by creating AI-driven voices that were not only realistic but also customizable to a wide range of applications. Their vision was to cater to diverse needs, from entertainment to assistive technologies.

AI strategy: Their strategy focused on developing advanced AI algorithms capable of generating lifelike and diverse voice outputs. This involved training their AI models on extensive datasets to capture a wide range of vocal nuances and languages.

Impact on productivity and competitiveness: The introduction of AI-enabled voice synthesis tools by ElevenLabs rapidly positioned them as innovators in the market. Their technology's ability to produce high-quality, customizable voices led to a surge in demand, propelling the company to a billion-dollar valuation in just two years.

AI tools used: ElevenLabs leveraged generative AI models, particularly in the realm of deep learning and neural networks, to create their synthetic voices. These tools allowed for the generation of voices that were not only realistic but could also be tailored to specific user preferences and applications.

Lessons and insights from Universal Robots and ElevenLabs cases, Embracing AI for enhanced collaboration and innovation

Universal Robots: Augmenting human workforce with AI

- **Lesson: Harmonizing AI with human skills:** Universal Robots' journey underscores the importance of AI in enhancing human capabilities rather than replacing them. Their robots, equipped with AI, demonstrate how technology can work in harmony with human workers, leading to increased efficiency and safer work environments.

- **Insight: Flexibility and adaptability in AI solutions:** The success of Universal Robots highlights the need for AI solutions to be flexible and adaptable. Their AI-enhanced robots can be reprogrammed and adjusted for various tasks, showcasing the versatility required in dynamic manufacturing settings.

ElevenLabs: Pioneering in AI-Driven voice technology

- **Lesson: Filling market gaps with AI innovation:** ElevenLabs identified a niche in voice synthesis technology and filled it with their AI-driven solution. This exemplifies the potential of AI to not just improve existing solutions but to create entirely new market opportunities.

- **Insight: Customization as a key differentiator:** The ability of ElevenLabs' AI technology to produce highly customizable and realistic voices sets them apart in the market. This level of customization, driven by AI, caters to a wide range of applications, demonstrating the broad potential of AI across various sectors.

Strategic AI integration: A pathway to transformation

- **Lesson: AI as a driver of competitive advantage:** Both companies have shown that strategic integration of AI can significantly enhance a company's competitive edge. By leveraging AI in unique ways, they have not only improved their operational efficiency but also created new value propositions in their respective industries.

- **Insight: Importance of a clear AI vision and strategy:** The success of these companies underscores the importance of having a clear vision and strategy for AI integration. This involves understanding the specific challenges and opportunities within an industry and tailoring AI solutions to address them effectively.

Augmenting human capabilities and creating market-driven solutions: Human-Centric AI solutions

- **Lesson: AI as an augmentation tool:** Both cases illustrate that the most effective use of AI is as a tool to augment and enhance human capabilities, not to replace them. This approach ensures that AI solutions add value to human efforts, leading to more sustainable and accepted integration.

- **Insight: Market-driven AI development:** The development of AI solutions should be driven by market needs and user-centric approaches. Both companies have demonstrated how understanding and responding to market demands with AI can lead to successful and impactful solutions.

Conclusion: Inspiring a New Wave of AI-Driven Transformation

These case studies serve as beacons for businesses embarking on their AI transformation journey. They exemplify how AI, when strategically integrated and aligned with human and market needs, can drive significant advancements, innovation, and economic growth across industries.

Call to Action

As we reflect on the journey through "AI Transformation, Ensuring Human Priorities in the Age of Automation," several pivotal themes have crystallized, each playing a crucial role in shaping the future landscape of AI in business and society.

AI as a transformative force: AI's role extends far beyond a mere technological upgrade; it's a transformative force reshaping the very fabric of business operations and societal interactions. Its influence is profound, ranging from enhancing customer engagement through personalized experiences to revolutionizing backend processes for increased efficiency. AI's ability to analyze and interpret vast amounts of data is not just a business advantage but a paradigm shift in decision-making and strategic planning.

The primacy of a Human-Centric approach: The cornerstone of successful AI integration lies in its human-centric approach. This philosophy emphasizes the importance of designing and implementing AI solutions that prioritize human values, needs, and ethical considerations. It's about ensuring that AI serves to augment human capabilities, improve quality of life, and uphold the dignity and rights of individuals. This approach is crucial in navigating the complex ethical terrain of AI, addressing concerns around privacy, bias, and the broader societal impact of automation.

Scandinavian Leadership as a model: The principles of Scandinavian leadership – characterized by egalitarianism, a focus on employee well-being, and a balanced approach to technology – emerge as a beacon for guiding AI transformation. These values advocate for a leadership style that is inclusive, forward-thinking, and responsible. They encourage a culture where technology is used not just for economic gain but for societal betterment, where employees are valued as key stakeholders in the AI journey, and where long-term sustainability is prioritized over short-term gains.

Embracing change and fostering continuous learning: The path of AI transformation is one of continuous evolution. It demands an organizational culture that is adaptable, open to change, and committed to lifelong learning. This involves not only staying abreast of technological advancements but also fostering a mindset that is resilient, curious, and innovative. Organizations must cultivate an environment where experimentation is encouraged, failures are viewed as learning opportunities, and employees are empowered to develop new skills and perspectives.

Building an AI-Supportive culture and education: The successful integration of AI into business practices hinges on the development of a supportive culture and comprehensive education programs. This entails creating awareness about the potential and limitations of AI, providing training programs that span technical skills and ethical considerations, and fostering a workplace environment that encourages collaboration between humans and AI systems. It's about building a workforce that is not only technically proficient but also ethically aware and emotionally intelligent.

Navigating ethical considerations and compliance: As AI becomes more ingrained in our daily lives, navigating its ethical implications and ensuring compliance with regulatory standards becomes paramount. This includes addressing challenges such as data privacy, algorithmic transparency, and the equitable use of AI. Businesses must take a proactive stance in implementing ethical AI practices, ensuring that their AI systems are fair, transparent, and accountable. This involves regular audits, stakeholder engagement, and a commitment to continuous improvement in ethical AI practices.

The journey towards AI transformation is multifaceted and complex, yet filled with immense potential for positive change. It calls for a thoughtful and strategic approach, one that balances technological advancement with human values, ethical considerations, and a commitment to lifelong learning and adaptation. As we embrace this transformative journey, we pave the way for a future where AI not only drives business innovation but also contributes to a more equitable, efficient, and humane world.

Embrace AI transformation

As we stand at the threshold of a new era defined by AI-driven innovation, it is imperative for us to not only understand but actively embrace the transformation that AI brings. This section extends an invitation and guidance to readers on how to effectively integrate AI into their professional and personal realms.

Think Big, Start Small: Embarking on the AI journey requires a blend of visionary thinking and pragmatic action. Envision the transformative potential of AI in your business – imagine the possibilities of enhanced efficiency, innovation, and customer engagement. However, pair this vision with a pragmatic approach. Start with small, focused AI projects that address specific business challenges or opportunities, this could be quick wins. This allows for manageable experimentation and learning, setting the stage for larger-scale implementation in the future.

Cultivate a culture of innovation and adaptability: To truly harness the power of AI, foster a workplace culture that values innovation, adaptability, and continuous learning. Encourage your teams to experiment with AI solutions and learn from both successes and failures. This cultural shift should emphasize flexibility and the willingness to adapt strategies as new AI technologies and applications emerge. It's about creating an environment where employees are not just receptive to change but are active participants in the AI transformation journey.

Invest in your human capital: The successful integration of AI is as much about people as it is about technology. Invest in training and development programs that equip your workforce with the necessary skills to work alongside AI. This includes not only technical training in AI and data science but also education in areas such as ethical AI use, critical thinking, and problem-solving in an AI-enhanced environment. By investing in your people, you ensure that your workforce is not only capable of leveraging AI tools but also of driving innovation and ethical AI practices.

Lead with values and ethical principles: As you integrate AI into your business operations, ensure that your AI initiatives are grounded in your core values and ethical principles. This involves prioritizing AI projects that not only drive business success but also align with broader societal values and contribute positively to the community. Engage in transparent and ethical AI practices, ensuring that your AI solutions are fair, unbiased, and respectful of privacy and human rights.

Stay informed and agile: The AI landscape is rapidly evolving, with new developments and breakthroughs emerging constantly. Stay informed about the latest trends, research, and best practices in AI. Attend conferences, participate in forums, and engage with the AI community. This ongoing education will enable you to make informed decisions and remain agile, adapting your AI strategies to leverage emerging opportunities and mitigate potential risks.

Engage in ethical and societal dialogues: Be an active participant in conversations around the ethical use and societal impact of AI. This involves not only adhering to regulations and standards but also engaging with various stakeholders – including employees, customers, and industry peers – to discuss and address the broader implications of AI. By doing so, you contribute to the development of responsible AI practices and help shape a future where AI is used for the greater good.

Embracing AI transformation is about much more than adopting new technologies. It's about envisioning a future where AI enhances human capabilities, drives sustainable and ethical business practices, and creates a more equitable and innovative society. As leaders, professionals, and individuals, our role is to actively participate in this transformation, guiding it in a direction that aligns with our values and aspirations for a better world.

Sources

Chapter 2: Developing an AI strategy and principles

1. Stanford Encyclopedia of Philosophy: Ethics of Artificial Intelligence and Robotics
2. Harvard Business Review: AI in Business: The Transfer from Strategy to Practice
3. United Nations/Nature.com Development Programme: The Role of AI in Achieving Sustainable Development Goals

Chapter 3: Mental blocks in AI transformation

1. ScienceDirect: Drivers, barriers and social considerations for AI adoption in business
2. Forbes: 11 Challenges Of Adopting AI In Business
3. Business Tech Weekly: Breaking Down Barriers to AI Adoption
4. McKinsey: AI adoption advances, but foundational barriers remain
5. Forbes: Barriers To AI Adoption

Chapter 4: Identification AI projects

1. LinkedIn; How AI Can Solve Your Business Problems: A Guide
2. Forbes: Seven Steps To Determine Whether AI Fits Into Your Business Workflow
3. Harvard Business Review: When Should You Use AI to Solve Problems?

4. Datafloq: How AI can Solve Business Problems? Here's What You Need to Know
5. Deloitte: Solve business problems with AI
6. Built In: AI In Retail & E-Commerce: 18 Examples to Know
7. Akkio: Revolutionizing Inventory Management: The Power of AI
8. AI Time Journal: Revolutionizing Retail: The Impact of AI on Customer Experience, Inventory Management, and Marketing
9. Linnworks: AI inventory management: 9 ways AI can streamline inventory control

Chapter 5: Choosing the right AI project

1. Harvard Business Review: How to Set Your AI Project Up for Success
2. TechTarget: How businesses can measure AI success with KPIs

Chapter 6: Prioritization AI transformation

1. Harvard Business Review: From Prediction to Transformation
2. MIT Sloan Management Review: AI and Business Strategy
3. McKinsey & Company: AI Proves its worth
4. Forbes: AI builds a better manufacturing process
5. European Commission: AI in Europe

Chapter 7: Preparing AI-Ready data

1. Expert beacon: Data Quality in AI: Challenges, Importance & Best Practices
2. Forbes: Data Quality: The Real Bottleneck In AI Adoption
3. GPAI: The Role of Data in AI
4. MatrixFlows: The Critical Role of Data Quality for AI Success

Chapter 8: Education and cultural change

1. ScienceDirect: Artificial Intelligence and its Impact on Leaders and Leadership
2. eLearningindustry: Integration of AI with LMS and HR for corporate L&D
3. workhuman: Empower workplace culture | Build culture with recognition
4. Springer: The role of organizational culture on Artificial Intelligence

Chapter 9: Choosing AI focus areas and implementation

1. Harvard Business Review: How AI Will Transform Project Management
2. TechTarget: 15 top applications of artificial intelligence in business
3. Deloitte US: Gen AI use cases by type and industry
4. Business Insider: How to Choose the Right AI Solution for Your Business
5. Forbes: How Businesses Are Using Artificial Intelligence In 2024

Chapter 10: The future of AI in business

1. TechTarget: 10 top AI and machine learning trends for 2024
2. Forbes Advisor: 24 Top AI Statistics & Trends In 2024
3. MIT Technology Review: What's next for AI in 2024
4. Gartner: What's New in Artificial Intelligence from the 2023 Gartner Hype Cycle
5. MIT Sloan Review: Five Key Trends in AI and Data Science for 2024

Chapter 11: New trends and challenges in AI

1. TechTarget: 10 top AI and machine learning trends for 2024
2. MIT Sloan Review: Five Key Trends in AI and Data Science for 2024
3. MIT Technology Review: What's next for AI in 2024
4. MIT Technology Review: Four trends that changed AI in 2023